Cable Factory 20

Lytle Shaw

atelos

5

Acknowledgments

Previous versions of parts of this book have appeared in *Mirage Period(ical)*, *Log*, *Lyric&*, and *Proliferation*. Thanks to their editors: Dodie Bellamy and Kevin Killian; Edmund Berrigan and Noel Black; Avery Burns; Mary Burger and Chris Vitiello.

$\ddagger$ Atelos

A Project of Hip's Road
Editors: Lyn Hejinian & Travis Ortiz
Original Page Design: Lytle Shaw
Typesetting and Design: Travis Ortiz
Cover Design: Ree Hall

Cover image: Robert Smithson, stills from *Spiral Jetty*, 1970.
Permission: John Weber Gallery, New York.

Cable Factory 20

0.1

       Everyone loves cable.
       Continents connected, sea-floor cable.
       The new cable lined in any neighbor-
hood.
       One *can* be embarrassed by the factory.
Description factory, tractor celebration.
       What role then for broad production
today?
       How to and the glamour of public trans-
port.

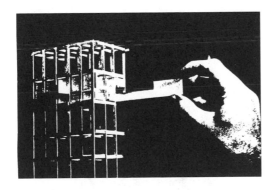

0.2

This way site would have
the broadest stretch.

Drawing zig-zag brick pat-
terns and etched street designs in yet
to be watered suburbs.

All links pressure skin.

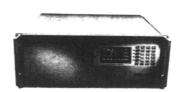

0.3

Which begs, who's the filter feeder?
Down at the bottom of the tank.
Connections, infections, language baths
(as the scientists and many poets remind us), may
not be what is distinctive or essential.
Sorting can go on indefinitely.

0.4

Could reference just fade back into the world, so excited to be at work and pointing?

Undergirding the lake and its extensions are cable's two modes—communicative and structural.

Letters man the fill.

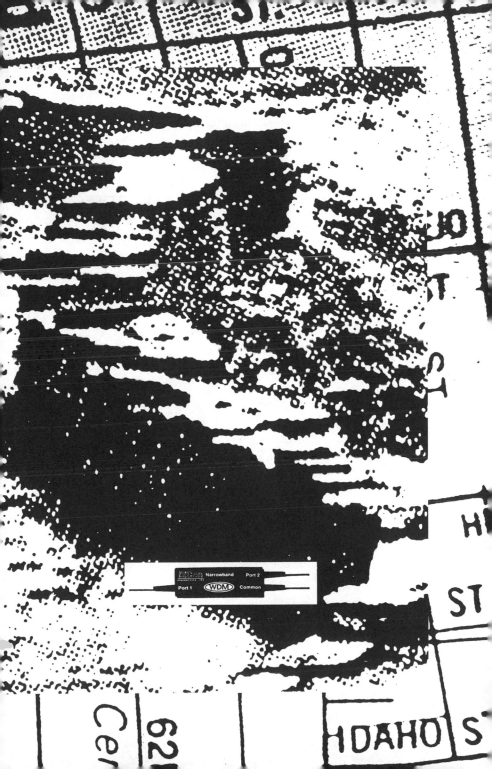

#1

Mostly it's small displacements:
      visual mining now heard.
      Cows bend
up from glass plates,
      chew on, learning to
diagram sediment, spin
screen room reels.

At first admit the fan.
Likeness dominates.
To participate, I draw scenes:
      life in Utah: a dump-truck
contest where picnics work
rock expansion. So hagiography
      deposits
yields in shallow water,
sinking to place
toward staked markers.

      This way
analog delay grows
      historical,
lodging specimens
      in fantasies
      of collapse never ours.
Searing in desert heat,
      a pickup
reverses—legs dangle
      over sand.

Only from the helicopter
     ochre designs
connect as plates:
klieg lights of noon-day sunshine
sap, cinematize the site.

Which is exactly where, since maps
at once crease to opposites?
     Bits thread west, others
to clean views (stores)
     and signal out again.
     Location leaps cleaning
     and suds apply
ear pressure, ear to ground.
     Out pencil-case.
Raise mud museum:
     send round word of where to saw.

#2

Mechanics drop tools to gaze at the nebula.
U-turning trucks pause in erosion beds.
Dumping loads letters for microscopes.
Sulfur-water, pumps, ledge deformation.
At this early stage, each method seemed to apply.

But the grain of surrounding
            less resembles desert lakes.
And as surveyors break cloud level,
            responsibility and chaos
            pressed under a new highway system
            vanish into diphthongs at a pool.

Lifts accelerate the passing-under function, weight
            gone in slickness of floss.
                        You know,
        certain aspects of this museum can peel away
                        but the reality behind
            filters you to the Plains States
                                    just the same.

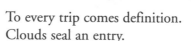

To every trip comes definition.
Clouds seal an entry.
        Industries emerge and jokes apply:
        a candidate for medieval knighthood,
        serving a knight as attendant and shield bearer.
Redwoods chopped, dragged to bay,
            nest and de-nest
        as debatable land claims monopolize port.

        Breweries become anecdotes—and now
You're watching from a front porch
        sprawl grown familiar:
Sometimes used as a title of courtesy
        in its abbreviated form
            after a person's full
              name.

These scenes wedge between blocks
And even the shellmound,
        forgotten,
        appears on recent maps, where
Lost intentions meet us on stairs,
        explain grocery lags. In short,
        air and land locked in vast lattice.

So as space widens, paths multiply,
      and breathy line-turns
      settle down to discrete camps
               (for bony plates)
      teased out in new
word-rooms of varying tile order.

See for instance the section on Henry Kaiser,
      three teams on
      steel hulls over hours,
          leaning on an exodus
          and changed group photo.
      Too variable!
          but looms still stream

Ramped streetcar lines link downtown
      to the elevated cemetery
          with a fine chalky deposit
      (perhaps dust blown from raised coral reefs)
      and oblong tubes spin behind glass.

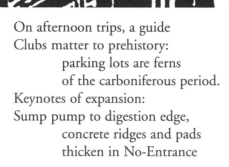

On afternoon trips, a guide
Clubs matter to prehistory:
      parking lots are ferns
      of the carboniferous period.
Keynotes of expansion:
Sump pump to digestion edge,
      concrete ridges and pads
      thicken in No-Entrance

Wound against the faulty naturalism
                        of cycles, like
Axel Paulsen, the nineteenth-century Norwegian
      figure skater after whom
      the one and one half turn
              jump is named.

Totality, in these early attempts,
      comes to advertise itself
      more like a small city,
Everywhere swarming with obsolescence,
Ripe as flesh eaters walked
      on their hind legs
          using their fore limbs
             for grabbing prey.

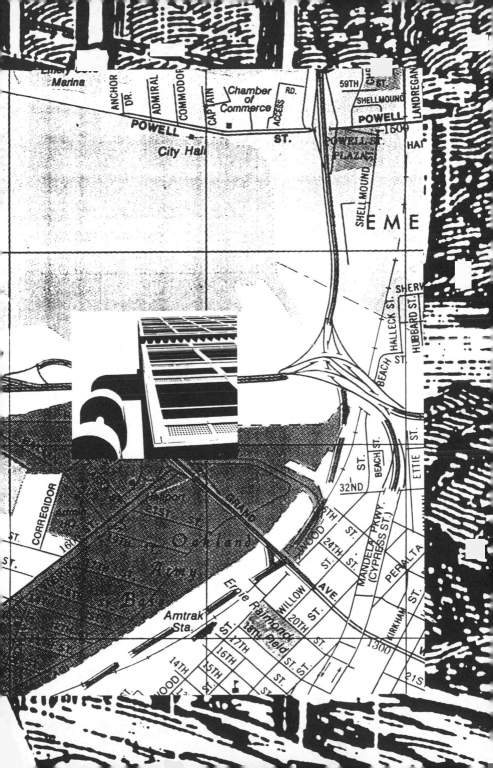

     Each city is actually a twin
      with the city of "Environs," where
motion propels into a phrase
universe whose quality of surrounding
(dings in the envelope but in tact,
studs and mortar bend to loading)

allows suffixes, abrasion.
     And from here, the twin evils:
       (disbelief in substance,
        the body as final container)
     appear as so many programmatic
         whiffs.
Look: I'm no longer to speak
     and the vocal moment
Trails in material.
     What pristine conifer survives?

Clenched this way, toothy indices
rustle up converts for the new
     theater of skin and its marks.
        Glass bits,
yards undermined or risk goes
slack on the reassurance churn.
     From these painted backdrops
     the Scientist enters to gasps,
        brings
toggles for sight machines

and an armload of declaratives.
　　　　Outer coordinates
leave the columns in an immense
　　　　roundness and vocal thongs
　　　　inside technical evacuations
　　　　　　　　of the agent
secretly emerge as a training ground
　　　　for sounding The Man.
　　　　Could he—then, could I?—
rush the approach, stroll into
　　　　a parking lot and find it

　　　　there,
ostention in gumbo mud. To rush
　　　　took on a new enthusiasm—
　　　　the return to the city:
cords trailing, zigzagged for
kneaded mounds—down to
scale and ascent, where
　　　　a dislocation point

widens. Now in rummaging,
　　　　now taught,
allowed latitude, brought
　　　　inside
toward lattice—a growth principle
(except centrality
　　　　and tonsures), so
right, he might have.

#4

"The documentary power
of photography
     discloses
          a succession
of changing
     land
          masses
within
     the park's

          limits."
    —An American artist

Men of fashion always pose (walking stick
     to terrarium and display)
     operations of industry as Satan's work.
     The park—a theater of addictions
     drawn on educational scenes.
Under each tree learn names:
     a transcendentalist practices benevolence,
     a teenager sleeve arms a bong.
Domes poke up from the city.

Some parks, therefore, exist before finished,
Anthologies of textured stone.
                    Transmitters radiate—
            circles—from points in the city.
            So to point took on urgency:
                            double doors
Lives displayed as volumes
To air-drum and narrate:

Crowds surround an annals refrigerator,
Returning to spread the linear
                    a simultaneity of condiments:
            To know how one thing differs from another
            To mark out everything by its own name
            To hear words as the properties

        Of classes, instances:
Youthful and very baked
The Boy was cast into a stormy period.

        When we arrived, clouds shut prospects
                    and stones came close
So that a walker lost direction,
Training with small explosions.
A moose silhouette stalks hill houses
Lending statuary a family
Sentiment

Roughly that: before impounded,
                              the goats
          were a great nuisance, eating
          foliage of the park's few trees.
Or were the stone markers
          properly extreme,
Carriers of the unexpected and of contradiction?
Knell tones—brackish
Summoned on holidays, so that
          our suited stroller begs:

What's lacking in this picture—
Allowances,
The sentiment of abrasion?
Eyes catch and toast is casual but
          a weakness in the eyes kept him
          from books, and he formed the habit
          of rambling about the countryside by himself:
                    in a mausoleum
          windowed trees and light
                    are figures
          for the permeability of shells,
Ready contents in the new language
          of extreme joints
          and partial correspondence.

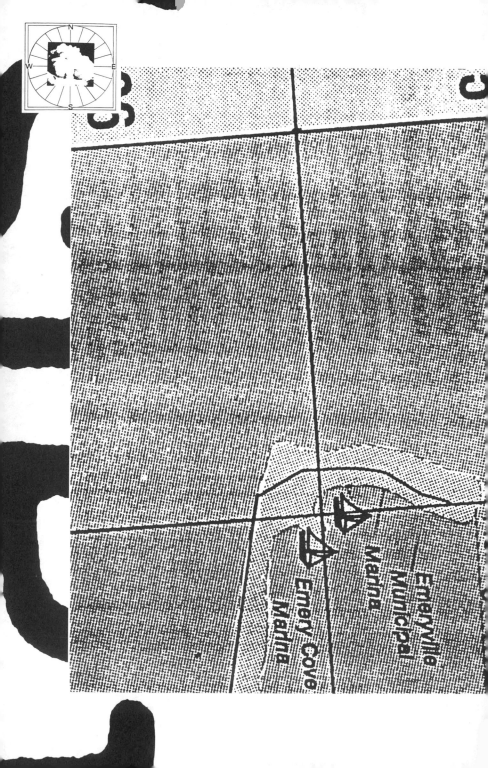

#5 Useful Information:
Parallels

Match

Useless
Unbind size: positivism.

Describe
During the process, writing emerges through a withered, ironic category of time (entropy) and shifts itself into space through an emptying.

Shores
Scale and historical argument overwhelm size and time.

Art
And so one walks in a present doubly absent, elapsing and trying to vanish toward inaccessible pasts, themselves unrealized, utopian futures.

Lake

31

Take

The site acts upon the observer with a barrage of sense data, pleasurable duress when distant geological periods overlap with the present in temporal collapse.

Cutoff

Creating a larger context for the work by substituting horizontal genres: detective fiction, geology, art criticism, hoax, acid trip, personal narrative, science fiction, technical manual.

Ranchers

Redescribe site as constellation of writing modes, cables to material.

Years

Stickiness

Sculptural and writerly temporality equal bad faith (liberal humanist progress).

Twenty

Temporal argument: a suburban tract home, a car dealership, an entire suburb each wants to situate itself on a particular future independent of actual time.

April

A charged space of contingent genres, imagined as an affirmation, replaces explanation.

Language

Scale

Space would emerge as the matrix of potentially combinable writing modes whose only governing principle is a pseudo-scientific tone that works to reinscribe agency a function of space.

Reflects

Object
Obsolete industry and advertising
become geological concerns.

Criticism

Know

Show

Windows
While site leaks time frames.

Armatures
Along with the overwhelming of cate-
gories and the aporia of sun-stroke, a
shifting of themes and spaces.

Tyrannosaurus
Temporality, now uncertain, creates
the context for an epiphany supposed
to generate the project.

Ecology

Road

Often we're called in to bind.　　　　b
Someone digs...and behold:　　　　r
marvelous extractions from　　　　a
under the subway: channel　　　　c
dredges, tow-trucks, cranes on　　　　i
slick overflow zones.　　　　n
Rookies have it end there　　　　g
which is why our technical

experience and the work suits　　　　c
win confidence on jobs:　　　　o
alluvial drainage fans,　　　　n
leach fields on the island: even　　　　n
themes, like the aspect of　　　　e
closure in rooms, or drawn　　　　c
　　　　t
radii in bulk diagrams, bundled,　　　　t
yes, at the ranger station:　　　　i
solid, impractical, even brittle.　　　　n
Therefore, love tales again?　　　　g

The brashness and air
advertise. But just what?
All scientific projections are taped,
leavened with odd voices,
seams. Push the identicals and they
rot, residue in uniform slots.

Offered, this way, as a signature,
can it stall objections to lists,
kickbacks and brunt,
schedules of junk pick up

where we might find the
figure abandoned earlier,
waiting at the service elevator
among frosts, exclamations or
trundling mirrors?
Evaporation powers circuits
recharging among the boulders.

inspecting

muscle

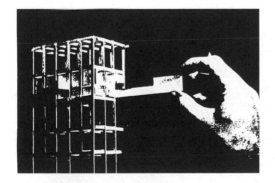

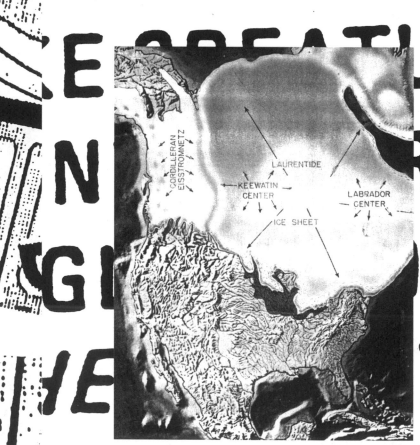

CORDILLERAN EISSTROMNETZ

LAURENTIDE

KEEWATIN CENTER

LABRADOR CENTER

ICE SHEET

Monuments could be that gripping,
          carved letters, temporality and
      winds above shale walls, insteps on black
Uplift creases along edge words, arm teams
      and organization of gross funds.
      For any natural wonder, explanations need …
         Nowhere else in the world
Did ice (here they come out with it)
      advance against override escarpment ramparts
      extending directly athwart the direction
         of glacier flow.
        In haze and perspective the two,
    caps and tall boots, recite
    upland stages and the scheme
       of east west division.

Students had loved these specimens. But the books,
        now packed in attics, await
      revivals at county libraries. You enter a metal
      roll-up door and add crates to existing layers:
        four hundred million years ago, the most
Advanced creatures on earth were jawed fish
      and this depth survey, principles and thinking
        in the hugeness of impersonal scales,
     coupled with the regional background approach
     populated the desk with a world
             of particulars:

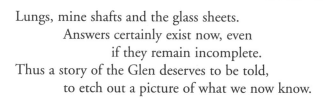

Lungs, mine shafts and the glass sheets.
        Answers certainly exist now, even
                if they remain incomplete.
Thus a story of the Glen deserves to be told,
        to etch out a picture of what we now know.

        First, the glimmer of catalogs, photographs,
        everything he ate for a month:
        writing the oranges and yellows
        of the digestible world, suddenly pulling
        back on the throttle and rising over bogs
        and clumps of moraines. Greatest of these
                feats is the
Creation of the rock basins of the lakes,
                two of which
        have bottoms (determined by sounding)
                below sea level.
        All of this increased the rural appeal,
            now managed from a vaulted studio
        over what had seemed the quaint buildings
            of the upper concentration.

Rooms gave onto the northern face
        tracing rain up the lake, as if
        squeezing had caused glass
            to pierce a white shell.
Yarns of residue strewn on banks
        and again the erosive competence of
Streams flowing parallel to the base of escarpment
        slopes confirmed the centrality
        of what had been gathered.

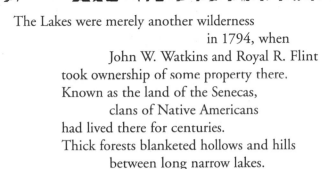

The Lakes were merely another wilderness
                    in 1794, when
          John W. Watkins and Royal R. Flint
       took ownership of some property there.
       Known as the land of the Senecas,
                    clans of Native Americans
       had lived there for centuries.
       Thick forests blanketed hollows and hills
                    between long narrow lakes.

Accommodated on rests, long shutter time
          turned water into a kind of icing,
          new substance better suited
                    to illustrate the forces at hand
                    like the problem of
Leaning on awkward first letters, a hiccup
          at some undetermined limit
          or a landfill of mined language for the whole
          three hundred and sixty degrees
                    in continuous lake
Some of it transposed across the country
Ready, if need be, to look close
          but
On examination he found that the jaws and clawed feet
                    were those of weasels,
          and the body had been covered with snake skins
          neatly joined and glued.
          This prompted a return to the
Crinoids, horn coral and clam-like brachiopods
          which dominated local fossils.

A study of forces elevated
Kinetic energy and some of the university theaters
welcomed the new business.
Slick footing and pools slowed the pace:
fatigue marks the point at which the soul
can no longer contract
what it contemplates:

Waiting for birds, becoming special androids,
one lost down stream in a boat crash
and the Lapps begin to question
the new blonde haired intruder
whose confidence in the face of the accident
reminds one of the subtitles
Accompanying his main texts, phrases like
ITS ORIGIN AND NATURE.

To bathe in several linked stomachs
what had itched earlier
in accounts
where the uncanny itself is
the landscape that resists smoothing,
its fissures and cracks attracting
sketch figures, arms raised
part in the thrill of danger.
Entrance was effected from the air,
gliding now that
Rents in the area would certainly shift.

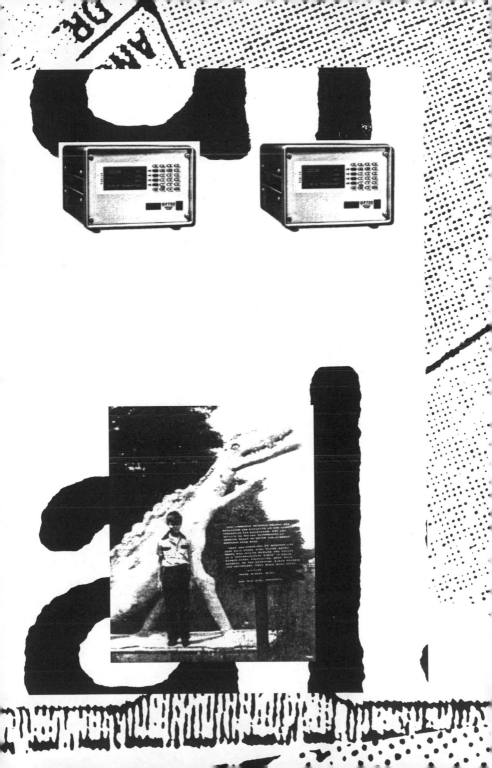

#8

Maybe bikers *are* targets, (so spiritual) tracking
Unnamed rodents along concrete, barnacled—a period
Drop off spot for playroom leftovers and
Sensitive men arrive in canoes, announcing
        the environmental

Angle: a dirt road along water deadends in highway,
Lifts and the eye-words of sand, potholes:
To be patient for sounds, like the wavering bell for ship
        tracking: high sound, the electricity
        in your brain: low one, the blood
        pumping through your veins.
Clips of hiss taken as social, the letting-in:

Rain, cars, wave laps and the gathering scratch
        of foot progress.
You select flies and bus roars for omission and in this
Summaries begin, the possible,
Tail in the air, diving for fish.

Anonymous treks in the wetland, never worrying if
        the nine year old will drown,
Left on frontage, nouning.
Smoke pours from a qualification zone, clumping
        above first start stalls. A club
Reloading to make his point, where the charts converge

On red clay. They had all liked this quality
        of graph-paper,
Covers even and the meeting joints. Now shops in
Königsberg had the pamphlets as well, rolled sleeves
        and bright light:
Someone would track the fluid from the hills,

Waiting for the six foot drainage pipe to spill
        at capacity.
Already the patch looks forward, tired of sitting
        and the unity
To sound, to notes, to stepping out to a place
        like the garage.
Each second slot accounted for with overlap.
Rarely had it seemed this extended.

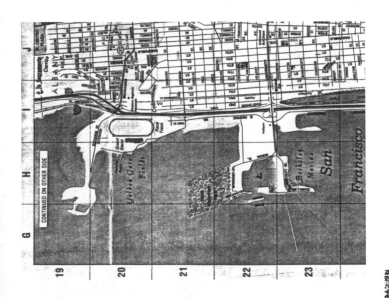

#9   Ferns of the Carboniferous Period

Mannered, in hats, but with a forward push
        an island of chemical paste builds,
      orange from the scrawl of trains
                   and recitals
         to foreign recognition in assemblies.
Usually he was embarrassed by this color theory
                  positive in light,
        painting the sheets, enough
    a stratum of the colored word. Wheels
Demand grounding in mass wasting
            and a national
        fascination at the rock-monitor's center
          grows enormous ears
           perched on moving water.

Silently, inside concrete, cores mine
        the jewel of content
   in laboratories, ducts and a lobby
   with whale skeletons,
                  the word
Aphanitic popped up in an elevator: finally,
     constrained by formulas all around,
                 the celebrants
     retired in privacy, followed
        the science of the particular:
Light, felt, as a space of precondition
          where
The colors are the acts of light.

A general feeling emerged, intuition
could put us in presence of *the thing,*
          grainy dumptruck fantasy
                    of rhyolite, andesite, basalt.

                    Clouds act force plays,
dumpy heater picks up
          riff, storage turns inside.
List granite, diorite, gabbro.
          Yes to pre-thought gowns
in sunk world confirmation.
          Salt licks strung up,
offered a playing field:
          traveled pathos, stare dissolves
current, thumps to hum.
          Along facts, nozzles and paths
from anthropomorphic issue:
          Left sum to interview over
unclip mikes, wipe
          samples passed round, truck
stored goods, gather for wait.

Radiant sky effects guide the process,
          encourage theories:

          Strata are acts of capture, black holes
          coding the earth. Work continues into
          the evening.

Now picnic tables and the spiny
give way to grouped:
fried food and winds from bay.
To walk through topics, hills imported
from Ireland
where contours are utopian
and houseboats wash up, pleated,
near the mindless danger of kites,
manned past legs on plush floors.
All a subliminal

Ode to the New Deal, only
trucks miss their connections,
tools left in the sun,
heaps of raw words:
impacted, massing and folded,
so that runners again approach camp
with clichés, then reformed:
bruised on the terrace by a fuller peering.
Voices amplified in empty space,
dammed by groveling. This vast basting

Continues along water ledges and in the streets.
Groups hone its surges,
campers emerge:
tent stakes, zippers and the slick
of rain protection:

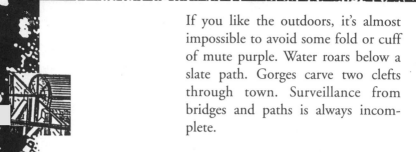

If you like the outdoors, it's almost impossible to avoid some fold or cuff of mute purple. Water roars below a slate path. Gorges carve two clefts through town. Surveillance from bridges and paths is always incomplete.

From this perch we see the
           sweeping ramps of the mineral

Kingdom, breaks in decorum like trucks
           or metronome laughs, the minutes sopped
                      in telling graters.
Slipping at jets, you refasten,
           brush a shoulder to carve space.

If, on the other hand, you enjoy
picturesque and imposing scenery
and have a lively curiosity about
the development of landscape features,
           family members could spread
                      without malice
               into their new, more private, rooms
               and food would taste more solid at meals.

The net result was accumulation
of bed after bed
of mud, lime and salt,
one above the other

Where, in the slide show,
the eye receives a blow,
and sparks seem to spread from it.
In some states of body, again,
when the blood is heated,
and the system much excited,
if the eye is pressed
first gently, and then more and more strongly,
a dazzling and intolerable light may be excited.

Attempts to shield it became impossible.
Exceptions swelled in the blue cordage area.
The shore at the cape became the edge of the sun,
a boiling curve,
an explosion rising into fiery prominence.

Stucco flaked from the facade,
dust swirled in screens, counting
jobs and calls so that
matter collapsing into the lake
enchained me
to an examination of individual faces.

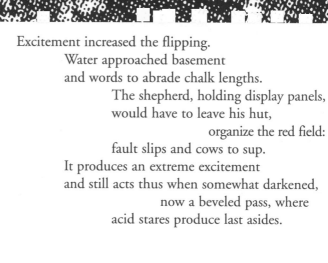

Excitement increased the flipping.
Water approached basement
and words to abrade chalk lengths.
The shepherd, holding display panels,
would have to leave his hut,
organize the red field:
fault slips and cows to sup.
It produces an extreme excitement
and still acts thus when somewhat darkened,
now a beveled pass, where
acid stares produce last asides.

Reverberations shake the trucks.
Lost in suds, Nintendo parks.
As the second evening came on,
I grew wearied unto death,
and stopped
fully in front of the wanderer:
from the sky plated face
emerged the viral yeti.

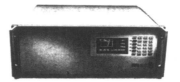

#10

> "This way to solar systems
> and rest rooms."
> —An astronomer whose nationality matters little

Managers bring forth
understudies, horn-rimmed
                                    glasses,
doodles from   electronics guides,
slide-rules used
            in

angelic fill-up boy
                        series—who are
left to imagine
            the light-connections,
twangs from apartments, offering
clandestine hints
            at beam origin.

            This we
Read effectively as
Yankees fan statistics,
            apply
second stage injector,
            lye development of
traced partitions, ink
                        on a topographical

assortment. Outside: overpasses,
linked margins of bituminous,
sand and cement—monuments
ravaged in the sun.

        Inside:
oxidized additions
        for scarred eyes—
counterclockwise sounding for
kelp deposits, tropical
        freight linked in
sections of pencil box.

        Behind: the cranes sway,
wavering at the door,
antennae operative
        for lunges:
to peruse shacks, mines,
                tonnage—
extrapolating from reversals,
requests and additions.

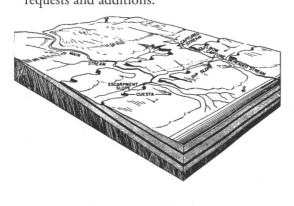

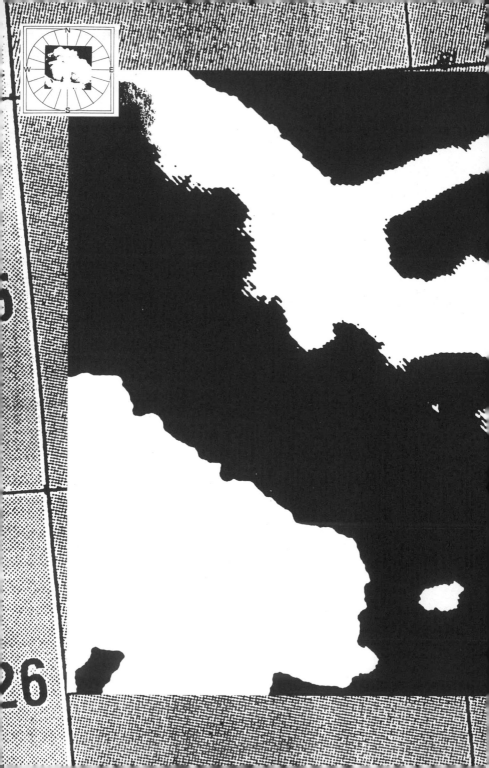

11

After the scrubbing

        only landscape   (M)
remains: (U)
          food and names.   (D)

Resolutions like: the slabs will not
sign lakes or street life eternally
but on a particular, say cloudy, day.
      You do it as equal as I do:

In an edgeless sun patch
organs filter chlorine,
bland bands streak and he
might drink the last Coke

anticipating hum. Now, not bound
by a Region's placeless (it)
or by old-timers colliding in Civil
War reconstruction uniforms.

Yes, someone said, postures
wither hand-holding contracts,
brain rangers on a lawn—soiled
shirts a flagrant display. So

(in this way) a Manager appears:
trod sensible shoes, and unopened
speak-mouth: such cussing
menaced the young lads.

A garage opens to slanted paving.
        Slats line and into dirt:
controlled by window seat, lake
        lines evaporate, bake as

capitals unglue—and you,
        making this work
of neighborhood gates mistake
pleasantness for tryst.

Note boats in park lakes
        raw sewage bubbles over
embankments and a handy man
        must be summoned.

Listings involve "the house" (its improvements); positions (posture, nodal points and power—envelopes for acts and their brain passages); walks (local architecture, planting and some hysterias). But all of these soon give way to a broader field accessible only by forgetting the house and the neighborhood, (though forgetting *these* and not other things).

Arms crash in water and heads bob,
       tile level rising in spit
as a bounce off plastic,
       time condensing to one

whose jaws fold down to accommodate
       large struggling prey:
an edge not digestion
       but incorporation.

So shag reactions face bottle rows,
       cavity wall stakes. Because
bikes stir air and you in there
       among the clothes investigating:

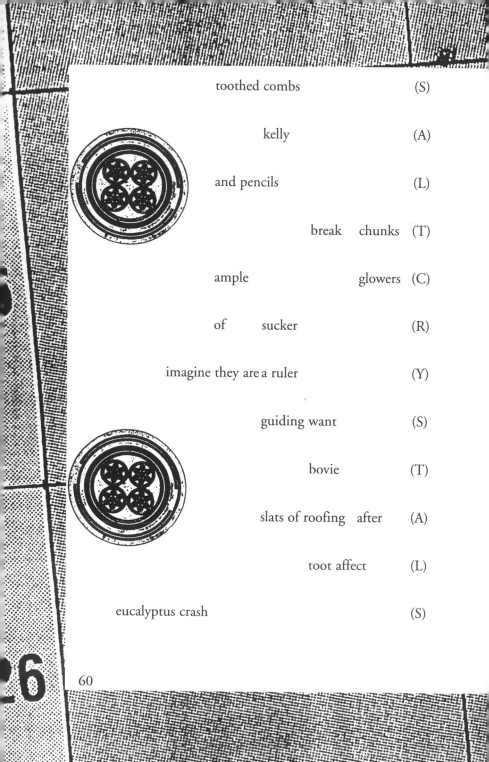

toothed combs (S)

kelly (A)

and pencils (L)

break   chunks (T)

ample   glowers (C)

of   sucker (R)

imagine they are a ruler (Y)

guiding want (S)

bovie (T)

slats of roofing   after (A)

toot affect (L)

eucalyptus crash (S)

(R)   These naps help—ringing
              dune tops in graphite
       from a bungalow's drafting board:
              I understand the fair as an engine

(O)   of population—now lead tours
              as issues of abandonment
       grow into business shoes
              loaded not unlike barges.

(C)   No day merges with telling inventions,
              bushes invisible in mist
       and in time no one is representative.
              Therefore each end a porch

(K)   on a study of exceptions, where music
              sculpts space into
       red bricks, air traffic and layering
              chirps, lowered in the eighties.

(S)   Brooding sentence trails blow off
              at loud inlets.
       Crows survey our flow path
              menacing the new additions.

Then, ostrich like, severance   (W)
settles: oval dresser. Smiles quiver,
rays exclaim. Waiting delegates position
or mumbles: as least as possible.

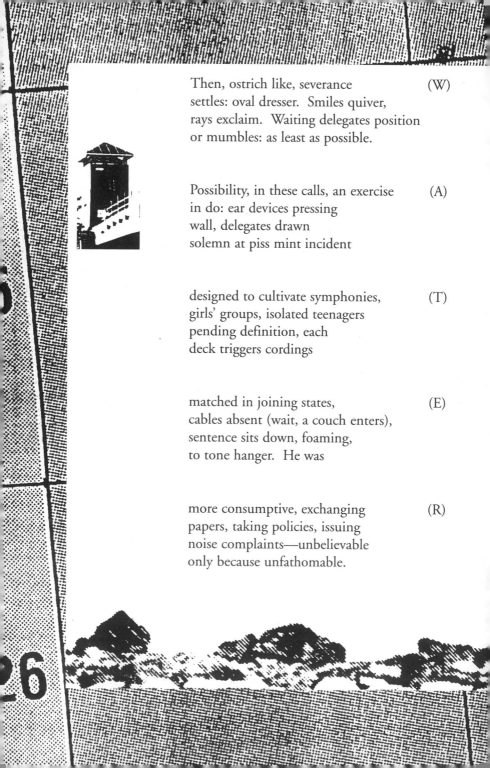

Possibility, in these calls, an exercise   (A)
in do: ear devices pressing
wall, delegates drawn
solemn at piss mint incident

designed to cultivate symphonies,   (T)
girls' groups, isolated teenagers
pending definition, each
deck triggers cordings

matched in joining states,   (E)
cables absent (wait, a couch enters),
sentence sits down, foaming,
to tone hanger. He was

more consumptive, exchanging   (R)
papers, taking policies, issuing
noise complaints—unbelievable
only because unfathomable.

#12

After I had listed the area's 22 best buildings,
I turned
to the shoreline guide.

All this time the largest cables remain
            rolled over.
Not the private roros
            (what the earnest call public spirit)
            but the aesthetics of rivets.

Now the peninsula to surroundings
and federal roll.

Would we call in a central body?
All locations on a single, seen in terms of.

Like the perimeter of a bay. Of linking.
For a shoreline guide: a matter of
            perimeter.
Objects gloss and categories:
plants, industries, public works, aquatic life,
parks, historical personages.
A font, a hand, a color of decay.

My apprenticeship involved little of this.

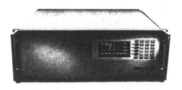

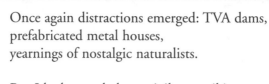

Once again distractions emerged: TVA dams,
prefabricated metal houses,
yearnings of nostalgic naturalists.

But I had recently been vigilant, striking out
4 weak cables. Returning to the project,
      I posted a note.   LEAVE OUT:

(1) Sound inventions leading to stories
      of aggressive and atavistic bowlers
(2) Plane travel and sea life
(3) The event in new age philosophy, parental
      cabinets, small scenes of New Mexico
(4) The attic as archive—a foil for military
      aquatic parks

Where would the project arrive?
No proposals lurk. No construction.
No rooftop exploded axonometrics of the cityscape.
No drawing at all.

The project is words and treated photographs.
It involves street repetitions.
Front seats.
Fingers.

In <u>The Native Races</u>, Bancroft writes:
> A thick coat of mud sometimes
> affords protection from a chilly wind.
> It is a convenient dress, as it costs
> nothing, is easily put on, and is no
> encumbrance to the wearer.

Thus, a list of materials:

Mess kit, Utilities, Draw bridge, Sea wall, Asphalt,
Linear perspective, Trowel, Cubicle, Radio tower,
Yardman, Shipyard, Telescope, Asteroid, Lunar
excursion module, Standard operating procedure,
Railroad, Orthogonal projection, Cement mixer,
Keel, Steelwork, Warehouse, Aluminum siding,
Truss, Elementary school, Rivet.

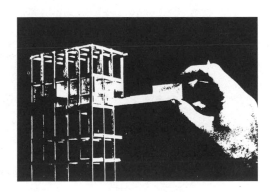

This began a drifting in powers: loss of
            here
Returned us to the roads
            WIDE TURNS,   lunch
To enumeration stretches. Staking
the train tracks, post-office, or tree lined boulevard.
In another poem, departure of the URBAN,
            fuels strict   tragedy

So we return to monitoring the stakes.
Left cheek warmed through
            a car window
            in sun across pier:

Hooks in wood, locked in events,
as if removable
taken off to a holding tank
where a captain, or someone in uniform
follows up on thoughts, your thoughts
                  (cartouches)
so any instance might build
            a boxed metal memory machine
            on an early train to the state
            for health and recreation

Like a pier: this wood and drawing
on the letters, on the number 20.
Not so much how they use it
as the arguments
it makes, through them
(a secret theory of objects, temporarily).
We walk until something occurs.

There, starting just South,
are the atmospheric conditions:

                              complete
                              and fragmentary,
                                      unearthed
                              during the excavation,

              of stone,

                              bone or horn,
                                      and shell

whose rain streaks include a maximum
of long sound patterning,
moving across hills
a body in situation has cheeks
hears Cantonese, mock opera.
In such light, cables not equations,
            gluing aphorisms.
In 1927 the pier was extended out 3.5 miles
so large ferry boats could dock.

The pier displays the bay:
land an exceptional
embolism in water,
cable a unit of distance.
In 1936 ferry service stopped
and the pier fell into disrepair.
One's mind and the earth
are in a constant state of erosion.

I claim a drone about elements
as memory machine to assert,
              to squat in:
         organizing, now, a geography
         of blimps, sailboats.
Mental rivers wear away
abstract banks, brain waves
undermine cliffs of thought,
         barely visible industry.

The water shored up the pilings and barnacles
that shored up the pier, that shored up
the memory machine. The mind shored up
thoughts and memories, that shored up
points of view, that shored up the swaying
of glances of the eyes. Sight consisted
of knotted reflections bouncing off
and on the machine and the eyes.

Like all mnemonic techniques,
like all guide-books, stapled
we contain our own liabilities
            in list form.

At 780 feet Cessnas, ship bells,
            gulls—our approach
fails to collapse us
into prehistoric struggles.
            We close our eyes.
It is remarkable that tobacco pipes
were found in this stratum.

At 2950 feet ruined E's vanish
into an abandoned penitentiary.
Round the brink of this hole willow poles
            are sunk upright
tops drawn together.
Bushes, or strips of bark, are then piled
against the poles, and the whole
is covered with a thick layer of mud.

Coming this late we simply list it:

Munitions, Urbanism, Dry dock, Soy, Altitude,
Liverwurst, Talcum, Culvert, Rudimentary theory,
Yoicks, Sea wall, Tonnage, Allegory, Limp, Sand
lot, Removal, Occident, Cyst, Killjoy, Surveillance,
World historical, Aftermath, Tableau, Eau, River.

#14

"Through place, the infinite."
       —A liar living close by

First, I want to mention banquette
          (here, sleep space)
    and marquee
          (music in the neighborhood)
    before the thickness arrives, as in
How string gorges, alpine streams
    and abandoned-car mud flats of bays
    along word axes drawn
    by suited slick daddies flying
        drafting board₃?

(M)

But the rapprochement was inevitable,
So I pretended not to notice,
    decided, in time, to bring the letters
        inside   the attic maybe
to pursue slip leads
    as the bulge
       of trash bags asks
           denominators
like
the space of the cab, fundamental,
     though not often pictured.

Unset, wake-up times expand in humidity,
　　　paper curls in piles
　　　　　and the eye-glasses seek
　　　daily practice in face thickness,
　　　　　　roped-off chutes for the potential,
　　　　　　　　where knots are negative
　　　　　　　and in time:
　　　　　　　　　him saying something like:

occupied with a late "crit," he and I,
his student, might glance up to find
his pretty young wife waiting at the
door to the drafting studio; a
reminder that life existed outside
architecture.

Down here, for instance, at the Frisbee golf course
　　　our utopian monorail plans
　　　arrive bound, bureaucratic green
　　　clashy accents carried off by traffic

Stumping us to write <u>Disturbingly:</u>
     <u>a precise biography of facts</u>
     or cede mineral ramparts
     of metropolitan park overhaul,
Arrangement farmed to planners,
Lock securing only itself, truck open:
     forearm relaxed on ledge
     forward, it directs, at trees.

     But withhal, the off-road sojourns
Turn up secretly beneficial, supplying
Characters like Captain Lars without whom
     the apprenticeship would have remained
     barren, private and self-imposed,
Revelation picking at its food, consulting
     the fourteenth nautical map.

You ask about the musical and pre-colonial
     periods, massive build-ups to popular
     patterns of lawn manicures?
     Our interns find only a band
     (too cool to be photographed).
So when rowdy lines drift off,
     each to its own (bad) television,
       measuring pads grow
     utopian again—and
Talcum restores the draftsman's ambition.

All the lawn seems tucked with stories
Lofty and stupid ones, taking numbers
So many interruptions—each a kernel hang.
       A train passes.
Recruits head out in that direction
       (owners trick poodles to distraction).
Officers themselves had sat at such tables, unsure,
       they loved to remind us, if their future
       would be with Tegetal, though proud
       of oaths, even

Concessions, like renaming the freeway
       after traffic victims:
Klaus Fluzoig Way, from an overpass,
       traffic speeding along the lagoon.
Slick rooftops after the rain, first since
       their return to the state,
              rushing out for
       the sudden heaviness in atmosphere:
         clouds weighing on high-rises,
           not quite repetition
     in pools
         which

Welcome the coincidence, crimes
          appearing regularly
As newspaper reading increases,
          institutionalized
          below the steady movement,
Teams having washed down the street
          before the hundred year parade,
Enamel on counters, drums suddenly
          in a blocked direction:
Recognition, they called it,
                    as if there were a before.

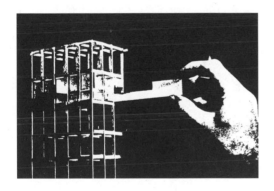

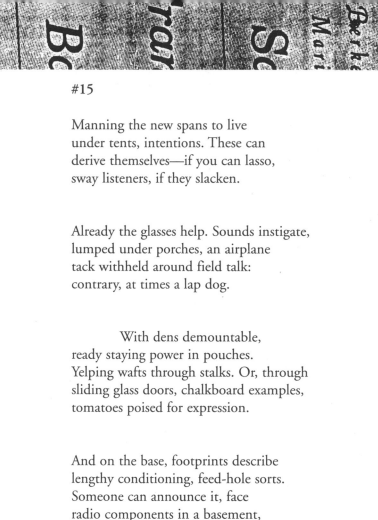

#15

Manning the new spans to live
under tents, intentions. These can
derive themselves—if you can lasso,
sway listeners, if they slacken.

Already the glasses help. Sounds instigate,
lumped under porches, an airplane
tack withheld around field talk:
contrary, at times a lap dog.

       With dens demountable,
ready staying power in pouches.
Yelping wafts through stalks. Or, through
sliding glass doors, chalkboard examples,
tomatoes poised for expression.

And on the base, footprints describe
lengthy conditioning, feed-hole sorts.
Someone can announce it, face
radio components in a basement,

or gather steam on the steps
clockwise its guidelines, cardinal.
   For squadron adjutants
keep expecting variance, thuds in
surface, stoking a furnace: file

while cargoes taxi, or modular units
appeal to commanding links. Water
towers over recently emptied blocks:
examples numerous, bland and fully
repetitive, or at least tail-gating.

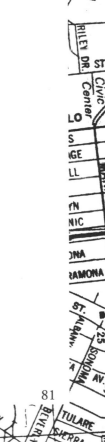

"We must choose true objects, con-
stantly objecting to our own desires.
Objects that we would select again
and again, and not as decor or milieu;
rather like our spectators, our judges."
　　　　　　　—A French poet

"I wrote on, curious to ascertain
whether this wild outburst of nature
could in reality oppress and fetter a
free intellect!"
　　　　　　　—A French historian

Distractions, placelessness and the hum
　　　　　of gone experience stretch in arrays.
To write bread, a candle—travel plans
　　　　　in gone medievalism.
Persistence is technical and wields
　　　　　the grain of enlargement.
　　　　　　　　　　　In fact,
Mounds rose to The Contingent
Under sound horns and outward buzzes.
Dumb blocks to hills and rain
　　　　　puddles on asphalt and tracks.
Sunk plywood and stains on a hung walkway.
　　　　I wrote, I noted, I compared,
　　　　I drew my own conclusions.

And thus I kept my intellect active, agile,
      thoroughly in self-command.
Learning from the aquatic park and
          its inhabitants, for instance,
    where the interstate flattens
               westwardness.

These are extensions for flooring which,
      not sealed,
   train vibrations fragment
   into fine dust on books,
          electrical equipment
Clumped now in smaller retail stores, chains
    wrapped in plush exterior green
    where just audibly over speakers
           begins
   a novel about going to the gym.

Routes gather the work table.
Yet even the installation of hydro-electric power,
     carried in abundance at low rates,
          was free of charge
    to any portion of the district.
So we might listen to a record, watch a movie
    and shine lights out the window
    simultaneously, since
The Great Western Power Company
         has anticipated
   these breakdowns in attention.

Almost paternal, the hand gestures,
        but inside this meant credit
        (just tack it together)
Like the new cabinets, historical
        connections balanced on one
Support whose movement can
        be confused with drips,
                leaving one

Ready to accept a silhouette of fence top
        palms as illustrations
        for the new vacancy, though
Our walks redescribe it, now
        the neighborhood, with
Cattle brand logos and checkered
                tablecloths,
        crisp iceberg lettuce and thousand
                island dressing.

Plain methods like
Keeping the same notepads as if
Seriality in the car trips would
　　　　produce this new sight, elsewhere
　　　　　　just a diffuse Americana
Which is of prime concern to the manufacturer,
　　　　　　so that
At length, worn out solely by fatigue,
　　　　I felt myself deprived of the quick,
　　　　delicate sense of rhythm.
The first cord in my being to snap,
　　　　inharmonious, over-strained—ruined.

In this way those seascapes mingled
　　　　　with the beautiful and dignified
　　　　　catastrophe of blocks
　　　　and I was left in awe of the
Early exercises in titanic mineralogy,
Revved, dyspeptic and turned toward
　　　　the state.

#17

Much of what passes as explanation,
under auspices—winged extensions,
dreams, satellite formations at
stalled ignition... The car goes

accurate and winged service,
lingering at pumps to place
taxonomies in side bubbles.
Clips are cartoon instances.

Glassy eyed jump shots
string you to a double drill.
For the post, this is an insult
and you must concede,
wrapped, as you come to be,
in brown snakes.
It's sunny out and early.

Our distortions make us solid.
This is why we're called
to sing praise, drip lead,
eject lightning bolts from our wrists.

Hello, start right in young man.
An endless variety of images:
toy hotels, tiny corridors.

Realtors lend instructions—at once
yielding to The Association Projects.
Some students protest, but
this direct talk severs none:

along dust the truck finds
landscape use, Instamatic
suns: pendant attention to stone
ringlets. So being bought

occasions sutures, tunnels
connecting street signs to rinds.
Keys connect and we're passing
slow, clear, a place you know:

wilted car lots, store fronts, tracks
as adjectives. Chains and wrappers
train futurity, in get-aways by
entry into commuter lanes:
right turns only, and elections.

#18

> "Once, when I was flying over the
> lake, its surface seemed to hold all the
> properties of an unbroken field of raw
> meat with gristle (foam); no doubt it
> was due to some freak wind action."
—An observer from any of several Western countries

Maybe it *could* be a guide to that unnamed ism whose finest moment is the abandoned Ultraist theaters and department stores.

Under commuter routes. Not realist or naturalist, the Ultraist accepts multi-cycles of the infinite. Styles branch and boulevards drain into highways.

Docks, too, loop in their own time sequence—containers fanning across truck routes and the devastated core.

Same time: new state and federal buildings wind in and out of residence hotels, fenced lots with small ponds in below grade corners, leveled foundations.

Anyone might explain. Walk up to the public viewing levels or have "strong opinions."

But belief no motive behind the timeless—an infrastructure that repeats itself in an infinite number of ways.

Clearly the walking part was given to chance. Or *when* exactly, like catching the "A-1 Piano Movers."

This way he does not 'make' history in order to impress those who believe in *one* history.

Then the rain changes color and flaunts degradables.

Sometimes a phrase comes later, only with enlargement—everybody at the party suddenly onto "Wigs by Tiffany."

Too much of it, though, still seemed uncovered—and this was what kept them reimagining the same approaches.

Asked for proof: a "Mediterranean" parking complex with an amphitheater of sponge yellow seats. Here, we watch a foundation slab grown-over with grass patches, trash heaps and several sealed entrances to what must have been basements.

Later—emboldened by what?—this movement became even more fanatical in its declarations, tagged a stanchion—50 feet up.

VX500 Low-Profile 1 x N Switch

U.S. Patent # 4,696,935
Made in U.S.A

Right, there is a cultivation of squalor.

One tends to get wedged in and the walkway deadends in Preservation Park where "examples" have been relocated alongside the existing.

Cleaning might go on indefinitely. Standing on a corner. Listing what doesn't arrive.

Knowledge wasn't the word that came to mind. Effectivity.

Such are doubly valued: spanning two thirds of known history and having survived the large eraser.

When I tell him I'm not, he asks, "Can I help you?"

And that summed it up, because we're in the center of the most intense image wars—while normally, one moves out for those gaudy—and often later abandoned—fantasies.

Terminal or whatever, you just order something and try to look inconspicuous.

Everybody, theoretically, has access. And of course no one is there.

Right in the middle, all by itself.

#19

> "The State is behaving like a malevo-
> lent Nature, whose meteorology
> knows only storms, cold fronts,
> cloudbursts."
> —A Dutch architect

Flakes rush in the cone of streetlights.

Tire squeals mean coverage and possible
school closings. Cars lose control on the hill and must be
abandoned to pulsating silence and abstraction.

To situate oneself in snow is to insulate child-
hood.

In a front yard, a shovel scrapes ice.

Before the war, I worked in a rock 'n' roll band.

During the winter months, we could practice in
the otherwise unusably cold parlor.

The problem of the proper name had not yet
been formulated.

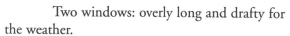

Two windows: overly long and drafty for the weather.

The house is full of off-white surfaces and looks bleak in the 16mm films from that period.

February and March stretch and one longs for the slow disruptions of

M
U
D

A triangular cardboard covering, secured at first by duct tape, withers and falls from the truck's front window.

Biography peers out.

As the rain continues, the smell of chicken soup pervades the wet cab, mingling at times with a nearby cannery.

Though the weather stars in several recent movies, <u>Drought</u> lends least to plot.

Inside a metal tent, windows rattle.

We sort noise into scales, block dance rhythms.

Panoramas reproduce the desk to itself. Minute variations span plans.

Twenty points. Books are maps. And differentiating thickness is not a matter of solidity, like comparing paper and

     With the force of no events, the project turned inward, speed increasing with the curves—as if any grip were a line, not a point.

     Bulldozers scoop a backyard.

     We could wait and, lacking glue, simply gather more materials. Eyes turn fuzzy in a department store and sound goes mono.

     But as the extracts pile up, small gaps, at first a cause of distress, gradually focus the application of hides, cornices and train footage.

     For instance: glossiness and the green of terra cotta; an Islamic entry way; then an overheard commercial—each drags guidelines.

     I'm not sorry I was fascinated with cameras and binoculars; that the wars passed. And galvanizing events had to be produced by will.

At night, the drain pipes creak. Before and after lack national backing.

What wilderness doesn't look (just a little) like a theme park?

We take trips into the city, sniff and consider. It's even possible to proceed from the air. Our lapses are encased in historical displays, sequential lights and a voice of unassailable authority.

As we work, the puddles accumulate and sounds have the concreteness of

W
A
T
E
R

#20

Variations propose a fix at root. Object stands impossibly still for a constellation offshoot.

For sight and word machines, a match at grain.

But grain surrounds—hitching corrugated metal sheeting, storm sewer grates, even a gangly cousin from the mountain time zone.

Linguists sought the internal relations that make language a system: a miniature Aztec ziggurat poised on the edge of an escarpment.

A belt of parks along the crest of hills, extending downtown through the natural canyons and along creeks.

The work surface grows weighted and splotchy.

M U D

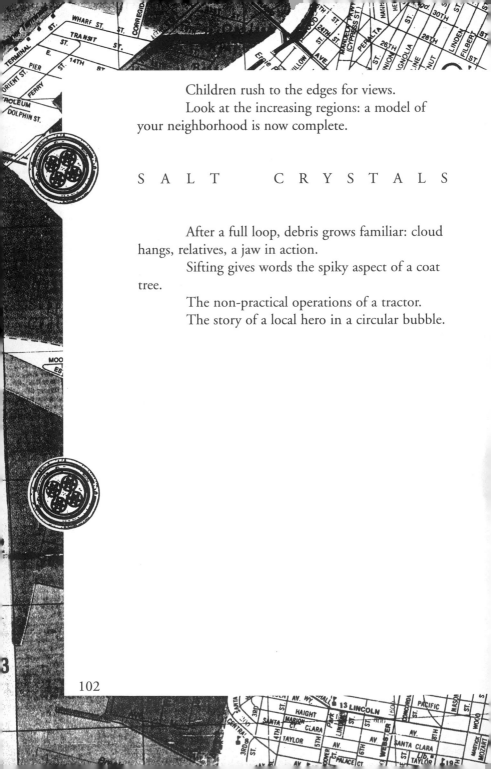

Children rush to the edges for views.

Look at the increasing regions: a model of your neighborhood is now complete.

S A L T   C R Y S T A L S

After a full loop, debris grows familiar: cloud hangs, relatives, a jaw in action.

Sifting gives words the spiky aspect of a coat tree.

The non-practical operations of a tractor.

The story of a local hero in a circular bubble.

Now the views have been cut down.
Toner checked.
The prosthetic copy machine redescribes the
world in grain. Does grain alert us?

R   O   C   K   S
              NNNNN   EEEEE
              SSSSS WWWWW
W   A   T   E   R

All week the in-between.
So steal them.
All that's left is to see clearly, to think, to con
ceive, and to begin again.
What city itself could direct us toward something
even larger, but controlled?

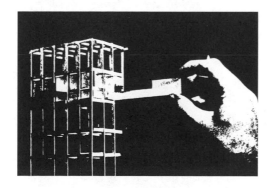

Research Materials

Asbury, Herbert. *The Barbary Coast* (1933)

Bagwell, Beth. *Oakland: the Story of a City* (1982)

Bancroft, H. H. *The Native Races* (1883)

Blunt, Wilfred. *The Compleat Naturalist: A Life of Linnaeus* (1971)

Cage, John. *Silence* (1961)

Carragone, Alex. *The Texas Rangers* (1995)

Le Corbusier. *When Cathedrals Were White* (1937)

Deleuze, Gilles and Guattari, Felix. *1000 Plateaus* (1984)

Emeryville Business Association. *Emeryville: Facts and Factories* (1940)

Goethe, J. W. V. *The Theory of Colors* (1810)

Koolhaas, Rem. "Architecture" (1985)

Longstreth, Richard. *On the Edge of the World* (1983)

Michelet, Jules. *The Sea* (1861)

O'Hara, Frank. *The Collected Poems of Frank O'Hara* (1971)

——. *Standing Still and Walking in New York* (1975)

Poe, E. A. "The Man of the Crowd" (1840)

Ponge, Francis. *The Making of the Pré* (1971)

——. *The Power of Language* (1979)

——. *Notebook of the Pine Woods* (1940)

Sartre, J. P. *The Transcendence of the Ego* (1937)

Shaw, David. *Watkins Glen* (1984)

Shklovsky, Victor. *The Third Factory* (1926)

——. *Mayakovsky and his Circle* (1972)

Smithson, Robert. *The Collected Writings of Robert Smithson* (1979)

Uhle, Ernest. *The Emeryville Shellmound Final Report* (1907)

Von Engeln, O. D. *The Finger Lakes Region: Its Origin and Nature* (1961)

Weschler, Lawrence. *Mr. Wilson's Cabinet of Wonder* (1995)

Atelos was founded in 1995 as a project of Hip's Road, devoted to publishing, under the sign of poetry, writing which challenges the conventional definitions of poetry, since such definitions have tended to isolate poetry from intellectual life, arrest its development, and curtail its impact.

All the works published as part of the Atelos project are commissioned specifically for it, and each is involved in some way with crossing traditional genre boundaries, including for example, those that would separate theory from practice, poetry from prose, essay from drama, the visual image from the verbal, the literary from the non-literary, and so forth.

The Atelos project when complete will consist of 50 volumes.

The project directors and editors are Lyn Hejinian and Travis Ortiz; the director for production and design is Travis Ortiz.

Atelos (current volumes):

1. *The Literal World*, by Jean Day
2. *Bad History*, by Barrett Watten
3. *True*, by Rae Armantrout
4. *Pamela: A Novel*, by Pamela Lu
5. *Cable Factory 20*, by Lytle Shaw

(coming soon):

R-hu, by Leslie Scalapino

Volumes by such writers as Carla Harryman, Hung Q. Tu, Clark Coolidge, m. mara-ann, Katherine Lederer, Rodrigo Toscano, Michael Davidson, Fanny Howe, Bob Perelman, Tom Raworth, Steve Benson, Kit Robinson, Craig Dworkin, and Jalal Toufic will be added to the series over time.

Distributed by:

Small Press Distribution
1341 Seventh Street
Berkeley, California
          94710-1409

Atelos
P. O. Box 5814
Berkeley, California
          94705-0814

to order from SPD call 510-524-1668 or toll-free 800-869-7553
fax orders to: 510-524-0852
e-mail: orders@spdbooks.org

Cable Factory 20
was printed in an edition of 1,000 copies at Thomson-Shore, Inc.
Text design and typesetting by Travis Ortiz
using the Adobe version of the classic typeface
Garamond.
Cover design by Ree Hall.